Original title:
Poems Under the Pines

Copyright © 2025 Creative Arts Management OÜ
All rights reserved.

Author: Levi Montgomery
ISBN HARDBACK: 978-1-80567-342-2
ISBN PAPERBACK: 978-1-80567-641-6

Where Shadows Rest

The squirrels strike up their dance,
While crickets plan their next romance.
A frog croaks out a witty line,
As shadows stretch and twist in time.

The bunnies hop with silly grace,
Wearing leaves as their headspace.
The breeze, it chuckles through the trees,
As whispers swirl, as light as tease.

Inked by Nature's Hand

The trees are scribes, with bark to tell,
Of chipmunks' pranks and frogs that yell.
Each dew drop glimmers with a grin,
Nature's ink reveals the fun within.

A woodpecker drums a comical beat,
While ants march by with tiny feet.
The breeze writes jokes across the glade,
As sunlight spills, in a shine parade.

The Harmony of the Woods

A choir of critters sings out loud,
With each note ringing from the crowd.
The owl hoots puns, a wise old chap,
While pigeons gossip from the map.

Breezes laugh, the leaves are swayed,
In this wild concert, none dismayed.
The laughter of trees, a joyful tune,
Under warmth of a silly moon.

Beneath the Shelter of Pines

Beneath the arms of towering greens,
The ground is soft with earthy sheens.
A rabbit slips on a wayward vine,
While giggles echo through the pine.

Bumblebees buzz with gossip to share,
While butterflies flutter, showing flair.
Each rooted joke plants seeds of cheer,
In this woodland world, fun brings near.

Secrets of the Evergreen

In the shade of the trees, the squirrels conspire,
Sneaky plans made, with nuts to acquire.
A raccoon in disguise, as a gentle breeze,
Whispers to the birds, 'We're the kings of these leaves.'

The pinecones are treasures, though sticky and stout,
A game of hide and seek, they're never without.
The owls are the judges, with eyes big and round,
In this quirky contest, high fives abound!

Tales of the Forest Floor

Beneath the great branches, what stories unfold,
With mushrooms like umbrellas, and secrets of old.
Frogs croak their wise tales, in a chorus so grand,
While the ants march in line, each with a tiny band.

The log's a fine stage, where beetles perform,
Dance steps in the dirt, a true forest norm.
A worm takes a bow, with the crowd in delight,
In this earthy theater, all stars shine so bright!

The Swaying Sanctuary

The branches are swinging, in a breezy ballet,
The trees take their turn, to whirl and to sway.
A raccoon in a top hat, is ready to groove,
While the wind plays the music, and everyone moves.

Chipmunks in tuxedos, adjusting their ties,
The forest's a party, with snacks from the pines.
Then comes the big twist, oh what a surprise,
The pine needles confetti, comes down from the skies!

Echoes in the Conifers

Whispers of laughter, bounce off the tall trunks,
The trees share their gossip, while gathering clunks.
The owls join in circles, discussing their night,
While the saplings all giggle, in pure tree delight.

The wind carries stories, of odd creatures' pranks,
Of frogs in top hats, and dancing tree pranks.
Echoes keep chuckling, with each rustle and sway,
In this comedic woodland, fun never will stray!

Portraits Written in Shade

Beneath the trees with bark so rough,
We make our sketches, but they're quite bluff.
A squirrel stares, with eyes so wide,
As if he knows our art's a bumpy ride.

The winds blow soft, they tickle our noses,
While pine cones drop like comical poses.
We laugh at the shapes our pencils make,
They look like creatures, all for a joke's sake!

Each shade we find is a world anew,
From tiny bugs to a frog in a shoe.
We scribble creatures, with legs looking strange,
As the bird overhead sings a song to exchange.

So here we are with giggles and cheer,
Crafting our worlds with each witty leer.
For in the humor of nature's embrace,
Our funny portraits find their place.

The Lull of Timber and Time

A picnic beneath a sprawling pine,
With sandwiches that truly define.
The ants are marching, all in a line,
Stealing crumbs, thinking they dine fine.

A nap we take, but snores interrupt,
As sleepy-eyed critters form a group.
They plan their day, while we dream away,
In a world where we laugh and sway.

A bear near-by picked berries so sweet,
He sneezed and tumbled right off his feet.
We cheer him on, then burst into glee,
"How clumsy you are, oh dear, Mr. Bee!"

So here we lie, in nature's good rhyme,
With laughter echoing through the climb.
For in this lull, we find simple fun,
As time and timber dance in the sun.

Musing in the Mountain Air

In the mountain air, squirrels play,
They steal my snacks and run away.
I try to chase, but slip on leaves,
Laughter traps me, oh how it deceives.

A bird tweets loud, I pause in shock,
Did it just say, 'Who's missing lunch rock?'
I wave my hands, it tilts its head,
I'm left to ponder, 'What's in my bread?'

Threads of Life Among the Pines

Under pine needles, ants march in line,
One drops a crumb, says, 'This is fine!'
I join their parade, feeling so grand,
Until I trip, now covered in sand.

The pines above give shade, not a trace,
Of sunlight-kissed cheeks or a happy face.
A chipmunk chuckles at my wild fall,
'Thread lightly, human, or you'll conquer all!'

The Symphony of Shade

In the shade of pines, a concert begins,
With rustling leaves and the chirping sins.
I conduct the chaos; a tune so sweet,
Until twig snaps loud beneath my feet.

Nature's musicians all raise a brow,
'Is this performer serious now?'
A cricket joins in, starts to dance,
'Keep it up, buddy, we'll give you a chance!'

Nature's Omnivorous Verse

Nature's feast is a wild buffet,
With berries, nuts, and bugs on display.
I taste a berry, so juicy and bright,
Moments later, I'm in a bug bite fight!

I swat and I swish, a strange ballet,
Nature's menu just got in the way.
The trees stand tall with their leafy grin,
'Eating outdoors? Let the fun begin!'

Veils of Green in the Evening

In the forest deep, I found a cat,
It wore a hat and danced like that.
I swished my arms, it leaped away,
Should've known cats don't like to play.

Beneath the needles, whispers flow,
A squirrel giggles, putting on a show.
He juggles acorns, never falls,
Until he trips, and laughter calls.

Tall trees sway with a gentle tune,
While owls hoot, both night and noon.
I joined a conga line of ants,
We took a chance, in leafy pants.

So here we gather, friends and cheer,
Under the branches, without a fear.
With silly hats and chips in hand,
In this green world, we take a stand.

Pinecone Memories

Collecting pinecones, oh what a task,
As I filled my bag, folks stopped to ask.
"What's your plan? Are you mad?"
Just wait and see, it won't be bad.

I painted faces on each one bright,
With googly eyes, they brought delight.
They rolled and bounced, a lively crew,
One tried to dance, but just flew askew.

At dusk we sat, my friends and I,
With silly pinecones that made us cry.
We told them stories, they nodded along,
Even when they heard the same old song.

As night set in, the stars came out,
And pinecone buddies began to sprout.
With laughter ringing through the night,
These quirky friends made everything right.

Dappled Shades of Pine Whispers

Under the pines, the sunlight breaks,
A shady spot where laughter wakes.
The squirrels scheme with all their might,
Planning mischief from morning to night.

One tried to steal my sandwich too,
I laughed and said, "That won't do!"
He chattered back, a cheeky grin,
With sticky paws, he dove right in.

A breeze picked up, the branches shook,
I lost my hat, it took its look.
So high it flew, like it had wings,
Turning my day into quite the flings.

As shadows dance upon the ground,
The laughter of trees is all around.
With friends gathered close, it's plain to see,
Life is a joke, and we hold the key.

Rhapsody of Roots and Sky

Beneath the pines, our shadows play,
We sing to roots, hip-hip-hooray!
The bumblebees join in the fun,
Buzzing along, they're never done.

A raccoon croons a tune so sweet,
As chipmunks stomp their little feet.
We formed a band, with leaves for drums,
And danced till our heads were full of hums.

With laughter flying from tree to tree,
The world felt light and wild and free.
Under the sky, so vast and bright,
We made our own version of delight.

Though our voices faded with the day,
The spirit of joy would always stay.
With roots beneath and stars above,
We crafted fun, and shared our love.

Beneath the Swaying Sentries

Beneath the giant trees so tall,
The squirrels have a nutty ball.
They chatter and they dance with glee,
While I just wish they'd let me be.

The pines wave like they've lost their mind,
Whispering secrets of every kind.
A raccoon steals my sandwich too,
He laughs, I sigh, what can I do?

The Green Embrace of Quietude

In the shade, I hide from bees,
Who seem to gather with such ease.
The breeze tickles my froggy knees,
Silly nature, oh, such tease!

A chipmunk hops, he thinks he's sly,
Wearing acorn hats; oh my!
He winks at me, then off he'll fly,
While I just roll my eyes and sigh.

Grove of Eternal Repose

In this grove, I lay and snore,
Barking dogs yell, 'that's a bore!'
'Go chase the pinecones,' I retort,
But they just wag tails and report.

The owls hoot gossip through the night,
While crickets plan their next dance fight.
Under this canopy, life's a jest,
Good luck finding a place to rest!

Under the Stars and Spruce

Stars peek through branches, all a-glow,
While I trip over roots, oh no!
Laughter echoing in the night,
As I try to run, but take to flight.

The pine needles fall like green confetti,
Giving my hair a look that's petty.
Each snap and crack sends giggles wide,
As nature laughs, I'm on this ride.

Lost in the Scent of Forest Air

In the woods, I took a sniff,
A pine cone dropped, oh what a gift!
My nose got tickled, what a joke,
I sneezed so loud, the squirrels all woke!

The breeze was fresh, the sunlight bright,
I danced with shadows, what a sight!
Behind a tree, I tripped on a root,
And landed face-first in a leafy boot!

The Stillness Beneath the Branches

Beneath the boughs, I went for peace,
But owls stared down, as if to tease.
They hooted loud, I laughed in glee,
Were they judging my tree-hugging spree?

A squirrel jumped down, felt quite spry,
It flicked its tail and said, 'Oh my!
Don't hug me please, just take a seat,'
And scurried off to find a treat!

A Serenade to the Green Giants

Oh, mighty trees, so tall and grand,
Your trunks are thick, like nature's band!
I sang to you, my voice a squawk,
You stood so still, like bored old rocks!

The branches swayed; I felt quite bold,
But then came wind, and I lost control!
I tangled up in lovely vines,
And gave a shout, 'This is not fine!'

Nature's Soliloquy in the Pines

In quiet woods, the critters convene,
The chipmunks chatter, oh what a scene!
A ruckus brews, humor on the rise,
As bees debated over pie size!

A fox in a hat, looking quite sly,
Rehearsed a speech to the passing by.
I clapped and cheered, made quite the sound,
Nature's show was the best around!

Patterns of Pine Life

Underneath the tree so tall,
Squirrels plot and pinecones fall.
One's got nuts, the other's scheme,
Chasing tails like a wild dream.

They dance around the forest floor,
Tripping on roots and yelling "More!"
Pine needles soft, the ground's a mess,
Who knew pine life was such a fest?

Birds squawk jokes with no clear wit,
A woodpecker that just won't quit.
While bunnies hop and snicker loud,
A pinecone throne for the laughing crowd.

In patterns drawn beneath the boughs,
The critters hold their annual vows.
Who knew pines were poets too?
With laughter echoing 'til it's through?

Journeys through Twisted Trails

Wander paths that twist and twine,
Where rabbits hop and pranks align.
A deer in shades of striped attire,
Claims it's just a pine-themed choir.

The trails are bent, not straight nor neat,
With laughter echoing at every beat.
A raccoon joins the silly race,
Pine-scented air, a friendly space.

Fallen logs like seats of fame,
The critters jest, it's all a game.
An owl hoots jokes, wise and spry,
While humor flies from tree to sky.

So take a chance and lose your way,
In nature's jest, laugh and play.
For underneath the twisted pines,
Funny tales are all that shines.

The Pine-Flecked Path

On this path, where laughter sings,
Pine needles drift like feathery things.
A badger cracks jokes, oh what a sight,
As he juggles rocks in morning light.

The squirrels giggle, planning a prank,
Hiding acorns in the old tree crank.
A crow, on lookout, caws and scoffs,
"Don't get too cozy, you might fall off!"

Each step is filled with nature's cheer,
A chorus of critters, far and near.
With every twist, a giggle grows,
Not a dull moment where humor flows.

So tread with joy and let it unfold,
Through pines and laughter, be bold, be bold!
With pine-flecked paths, the fun's begun,
Join the wild ones; bring the sun.

Atlas of Nature's Deceptions

Here lies the atlas, full of tricks,
Mapped with gags and nature's flicks.
Pine trees wear their bark like hats,
As squirrels giggle, 'Look, it chats!'

Every page twists with silly sights,
Unexpected turns and playful nights.
A skunk with flair and mischief grand,
Plans a fashion show across the land.

Branches wave like arms in jest,
As creatures bloom for the grand fest.
A lizard sunbakes, claims it's a pizza,
"Grab a slice, it's all a teasa!"

So open the atlas, take a glance,
Join the pines for a silly dance.
In nature's realm, what a delight,
Where laughter reigns both day and night.

Musing Amongst the Tall Sentinels

Beneath the branches, squirrels play,
Conducting concerts, loud and gay.
They gather acorns, making a fuss,
While I just sit here, join the bus.

A woodpecker knocks, a clumsy beat,
His rhythm's off, but he's got heat.
The pines listen with patient grace,
Laughing quietly at his pace.

A deer walks in, eyes wide with glee,
Looking lost like it's a spree.
Did they misplace their dinner time?
Or is this just a nature rhyme?

Among the giants, I find my muse,
Imperfect sounds that I can't refuse.
This forest life a joyful jest,
With every creature, I'm truly blessed.

The Breath of the Swaying Trees

The pines whisper secrets, soft and sly,
An owl hoots, a mysterious guy.
With every breeze, they dance and tease,
As if they're telling jokes with ease.

A raccoon lurks with mischief planned,
He spots my sandwich, thinks it's grand.
I shoo him away, but in my haste,
He steals my lunch with such great taste!

In the shadows, shadows play tricks,
Branches sway like they're doing flicks.
A chipmunk waits, a comedian's grin,
Waiting for applause, drops the pin.

Life in the grove is quirky and bright,
With laughter echoing in the night.
Amongst the trees with humor rife,
Each breath is joy, a punchline of life.

Rustling Memories of the Forest

Leaves giggle as they flutter down,
Nature's jesters in a leafy crown.
While crickets chirp in offbeat rhyme,
They're serenading this silly time.

A fox prances with a playful leap,
Pretending to be secretive, oh so deep.
But everyone knows he's just a clown,
With a tail that sweeps like a flowing gown.

Mushrooms pop up, wearing silly hats,
Surprise guests at the tree's chit-chats.
Who knew the woods could crack a smile?
With laughter echoing mile after mile.

Rustling memories paint my mind,
In this laughter, solace I find.
Each tree presents its own quirky tale,
A forest carnival where none can fail.

Lullabies in the Piney Deep

Under starry skies, the pines conspire,
Whispering secrets, fueling laughter's fire.
A baby owl hoots with all its might,
His parents roll eyes in the soft twilight.

The nocturnal critters begin their dance,
A raccoon and skunk share a clumsy prance.
With moonlight as their glittery stage,
They shimmy and shake, breaking every cage.

In the distance, a frog croaks an ode,
To the rhythm of night, in laughter bestowed.
Stars chuckle as they twinkle and peep,
These are the lullabies in the piney deep.

Joyful shadows hug the forest floor,
With silliness bound to forever soar.
In this wild pocket, dreams aren't cheap,
Just the heart's laughter — a quaint little sweep.

Song of the Sylvan Grove

In the grove where squirrels chatter,
A raccoon tells jokes on a platter.
Trees laugh as the wind takes a swing,
Nature sure knows how to zing!

Beneath the branches, shadows dance,
A chipmunk struts, as if in a trance.
Leaves rustle like a crowd of mates,
Even pine cones join in debates!

Frogs croak tunes, a silly choir,
Their croaks like jokes, never tire.
The sun peeks through in golden rays,
All watch the trees boast of their days.

Silly winds play tag with the leaves,
They laugh and tease, oh how it weaves!
Nature's fun in every way,
Beneath the pines, we all will play!

Dreams among the Tall Timbers

Tall timbers whisper silly tales,
Of lost socks and stinky snails.
Owls hoot in goofy delight,
As fireflies flash their brightest light.

Dreamers nap on beds of moss,
While rabbits share stories of loss.
"Who took my carrot?" they all shout,
Laughter echoes all about!

The trees sway gently, full of glee,
"Anyone for some acorn tea?"
Birds show off their colorful styles,
While critters gather in silly piles.

A bear trips over his own feet,
As laughter rings through the leafy street.
Dreams come alive, bright and bold,
With side-splitting stories to be told!

Breathing in the Canopy

In the canopy, the breeze is sly,
It tickles the trees, oh me, oh my!
Branches sway with a comical grace,
As if they're taking part in a race.

A woodpecker joins with a drum beat,
And squirrels perform their best dance feat.
The sun shines down like a spotlight,
Making every creature feel just right.

Here, no one takes life too grim,
Even shadows hum a little hymn.
Every creature's got a clever joke,
Even the mushrooms begin to poke.

In this patch, where laughter's grand,
We find joy in the leafy band.
Breathing in the fun-filled air,
Nature's humor is everywhere!

Serene Solitude Under the Boughs

Under the boughs, where giggles hide,
A wise old turtle takes a glide.
"Slow and steady wins the race," he grins,
As rabbits plot whimsical spins.

A ladybug dons a tiny crown,
While ants march proudly through the town.
Every leaf holds a secret cheer,
In this serene space, fun is near.

Beneath the shade, a dance begins,
As crickets chirp their raucous sins.
Laughter bubbles like a spring,
In solitude, joy takes wing.

Under the boughs, let's share a laugh,
With creatures gathered; a fun-filled staff.
Together we find sweet delight,
In this playful world, so warm and bright!

Evergreen Dreams Awakened

In the forest, where squirrels dance,
A pine cone rolls, it takes a chance.
A raccoon laughs, its mask so sly,
Chasing shadows, oh my, oh my!

A woodpecker tries to steal a show,
Tapping tunes, a real pro though.
The trees giggle, in whispers sweet,
While chipmunks plot to take the seat.

A breeze tickles branches, naughty and bold,
Making secrets that trees have told.
They sway and sway, with giggles loud,
The forest is quirky, it's never cowed!

As birds drop jokes from lofty height,
The sun peeks through, a silly sight.
Oh, how they play, these lively sights,
Dreams awaken in nature's lights!

Shimmers on the Pine's Surface

Sunshine sparkles on needles bright,
While bugs perform their bug ballet tonight.
Each gust of air sends giggles around,
Confetti of leaves falls to the ground.

A squirrel slips, oh what a chase,
It flips through branches, it's a wild race.
Laughter follows, carried by wind,
In this pine kingdom, mishaps are pinned.

A deer sneezes, a loud "ACHOO!"
Startling birds in a great hullabaloo.
The forest chuckles, with voices so clear,
Every mishap brings laughter near!

The shadows dance, in a playful prance,
Nature's stage set for a quirky romance.
In every branch, a giggle, a smile,
Such shimmers make the world worthwhile!

Nature's Cadence Among the Boughs

Under the pines, a rhythm flows,
Nature's band, nobody knows.
Toads croak beats, frogs sing along,
A funny serenade, nature's song.

The rustling leaves snap their fingers loud,
The breeze joins in, feeling so proud.
Each creature plays its quirky part,
A symphony crafted from nature's heart.

An owl hoots, off-beat and sly,
A nearby rabbit gives a side-eye.
What a weirdo, the woods all grin,
In this cadence, let the fun begin!

With pine nuts dropping like confetti rain,
Laughter spreads through laughter's chain.
Oh, in this grove, such joyous sounds,
Nature's rhythm where joy abounds!

When Pines Hold Secrets

Beneath the pines, secrets abound,
Stories shared without a sound.
A wise old stump listens so keen,
While critters conspire, a stealthy scene.

The birds gossip with feathers afluff,
While pinecones chuckle, that's more than enough.
A badger nods, oh so wise,
Hiding tales behind its bright eyes.

A tiny ant carries a crumb so grand,
It shares its scoop with a nearby band.
In the dark shade, whispers ignite,
Oh, what a tale under the light!

As dusk rolls in, laughter rings clear,
All the secrets that pine trees hear.
In this forest, hilarity thrives,
From laughter and fun, nature derives!

Beneath the Boughs of Solitude

Under branches, squirrels play,
Chasing acorns, day by day.
I sit here with my roots in dirt,
Wondering if I need a shirt.

Rabbits hop like they own the place,
While I watch with a grin on my face.
A bird drops a joke, it cracks me up,
I spill my coffee in my cup.

The wind whispers secrets, soft and sweet,
Tossing twigs at my dancing feet.
I'm the king of this leafy domain,
Where laughter echoes, free from the rain.

Oh, to be a pine in this droll retreat,
Waving to the trees like they're on repeat.
Underneath boughs, life's quite a show,
Even when nature steals my flow.

Reflections Amidst the Starlit Pines

Stars twinkle above in a cheeky grin,
While crickets hum tunes that tickle my chin.
I dance like a fool, not caring who sees,
Under the light of the night's gentle breeze.

I whisper my secrets to the old fir tree,
It nods like it's heard them all, just for me.
The moon teases shadows, making me sway,
As I trip on a root, hip-hop on display.

Fireflies flicker, my disco lights shining,
While I serenade nature with hummed, silly rhyming.
A pinecone falls, percussion to my song,
Who knew the woods could be this much fun all along?

In this gathering of starlit delight,
I'm a jester beneath the boughs, taking flight.
Each giggle and chuckle, a sweet serenade,
In the night's gentle arms, my worries all fade.

Chronicles of the Whispering Woods

In the woods, where whispers play,
I laugh with trees in a jazzy way.
The branch above me breaks into song,
Tune's gone wild, I can't help but throng.

Chipmunks gossip about my latest falls,
Clumsy moves and embarrassing sprawls.
The owls hoot their laughter from high,
Their wise, old faces, oh so sly.

Each twig tells tales of silly blunders,
Of squirrels and deer and playful wonders.
Nature's the host of this live comedy,
Where even the plants hold a grand jubilee.

Amongst the branches, under the glow,
I bond with the roots, and put on a show.
In these whispering woods, pure glee I find,
With chuckles and giggles left far behind.

Glistening Dew on Pine Needles

Morning breaks, dew drops twinkle bright,
With that glow, I'm ready to take flight.
The pine needles sparkle in the sun's embrace,
I'm a morning dancer, keeping my pace.

Critters lurking with breakfast on mind,
A chipmunk's laugh is the best you'll find.
They argue over the last crumb, then chase,
Each furry creature knows how to embrace.

I join their antics, flipping and flopping,
With a joyful heart that's always hopping.
Nature's a playground, wild and free,
Making memories, just silly me.

Glistening dew, your magic makes me grin,
Reminds me of play when the day begins.
With laughter resounding among the trees,
A light-hearted symphony dances on the breeze.

Footprints in the Pine Needle Carpet

A squirrel gave me quite a scare,
As I tripped over its fuzzy hair.
I laughed, I rolled, fell on the ground,
In nature's funny circus, joy is found.

The pines stand tall, keep watchful eyes,
While I attempt my acrobatics, oh what a surprise!
With every step, I crunch and slide,
The forest floor's my trusty guide.

Unruly branches tug at my hat,
A raccoon giggles, 'What's up with that?'
I nod, accept my silly fate,
Just a jester in a forest state.

So here I am, legs all a-twirl,
In this laughing woods, my heart's in a whirl.
With layers of needles underfoot,
Every stumble is sweetly cute.

Timeless Reverie Under the Branches

Under branches, I dream awake,
With all the giggles that I can make.
A bird sneezes, oh what a sound,
It causes laughter to bounce around.

The sun peeks through like a cheeky grin,
While pine trees fail at keeping it in.
I shout to clouds, 'Don't rain on me!'
They laugh back softly, 'Just wait and see.'

Breezes sway, my thoughts twirl and spin,
Lost in a daydream, that's where I win.
The branches sway like dancing pals,
I join their party, cause we're all gal pals.

As time slips past without a care,
Laughter echoes through the forest air.
In this timeless state, chaos reigns,
Underneath the trees, joy remains.

The Artistry of Evergreen Dreams

In the forest's embrace, my mind's a canvas,
Where laughter paints scenes, oh what a fuss!
Pine and poke, I weave through the green,
Each step a giggle, each branch a scene.

Nature's brush strokes, wild and free,
A masterpiece where I just want to be.
The trees chuckle softly, 'Watch your back!'
While a doe prances, my heart goes 'whack!'

The shadows play tricks, and so do I,
With pinecones hurled as birds flutter by.
Every whisper of wind is a playful tease,
I stumble through art, lost in the breeze.

Evergreen dreams, my giggling muse,
In this vibrant chaos, there's no excuse.
Laughter my palette, joy my theme,
Under the canopy, I dance and beam.

Reflections in the Forest Light

Sunlight flickers through leafy vines,
I dance with shadows, and laugh at signs.
Pine trees waltz as I trip and fall,
Echoes of chuckles, a nature's call.

The brook gurgles like a silly stream,
Each splash a punchline in my playful dream.
A bear rolls by, just having fun,
We make quite a pair, the giggly ones.

Nature's mirror's full of gleeful sights,
Reflecting humor in the soft daylight.
With every step, I leap and glide,
In this wondrous place, joy is my guide.

So if you wander where laughter sings,
Join the frolic, let joy take wings.
Under the trees, we'll laugh and twine,
In reflections of light, our spirits align.

Sighs of the Coniferous Wind

Beneath the tall pines, squirrels dance,
Chasing each other, no time to prance.
A gust of wind steals a hat away,
Leaving the chap in a comical fray.

A bird sings loudly, then trips on a limb,
Flapping and flailing, oh what a whim!
The laughter of branches, rustles and snickers,
Joining the fun, they play clever trickers.

But what's this? A pinecone slips and rolls,
Crashing down hard, oh the trouble it tolls!
It bounces right off a fellow's big head,
Creating a game of "who's really dead?"

Nature's jesters, under green crowns they lie,
Making us chuckle and wondering why.
With each little mishap, the forest does cheer,
For laughter beneath pines is always near.

A Tapestry of Twigs and Tales

In the shade of the pines, a fox tells a yarn,
Of woodland creatures causing alarm.
A raccoon in pajamas, a deer in a tie,
Together they plot, oh my, oh my!

The owl hoots loudly, a joker he seems,
Mixing up riddles and wild, wacky dreams.
A frog leaps too high, landing right in mud,
Turns out it's a game of who's next in the flood.

Branches above whisper secrets of fun,
Whirling and twirling, like leaves on the run.
A snake wears a hat, borrowed from a snail,
With fashion so quirky, it can't help but prevail.

The laughter of Nature, a melody bright,
Engaging all critters under starry night.
Twigs weave the tales, the stories unfold,
In this world of wonder, let laughter take hold.

Echoes of the Pinecone Dream

Once in a while, a pinecone will shout,
Rolling down hills, trying to sprout.
A rabbit looks on, with a twitch of its nose,
Saying, "Hey buddy, that's not how it goes!"

The breeze brings some giggles, a rustle of leaves,
Nature's own laughter just never deceives.
A chipmunk in stitches, can hardly keep still,
As branches above drop a ticklish thrill.

Even the shadows join in on the cheer,
As critters all chuckle, "Oh dear, oh dear!"
With shrubs in a tangle, it's mayhem and glee,
A pinecone's adventure, oh what a sight to see!

So let's raise a toast, with acorns tonight,
To woodland hijinks and all that feel right.
For laughter in forests brings joy to the scene,
In echoes of nonsense, forever we dream.

Secrets in the Woodland Silence

In the hush of the pines, secrets are spilled,
As chipmunks debate, the air still and chilled.
"Do you think that tree's always been that tall?"
The other one chuckles, "Well, not since the fall!"

Mice gather tales from the roots of old trees,
Whispering rumors as light dances with breeze.
A caterpillar snickers, in a leafy disguise,
Imagining life as a butterfly flies.

A turtle spins yarns, oh so slow and profound,
Each word a treasure, like jewels that abound.
Yet squirrels will giggle, the wise old mushrooms,
Saying, "You'll move fast only after the blooms!"

The sun dips low, casting shadows so wide,
While laughter and wisdom join side by side.
In the heart of the silence, fun marries grace,
In woodland enigma, we all find our place.

Verdant Whispers in the Breeze

Beneath the trees where shadows play,
A squirrel forgot where he laid his acorn.
Chasing his tail, he darts and sways,
Only to trip on a branch now quite worn.

A raccoon laughs from his lofty side,
Pointing and giggling at the squirrel's mess.
In a world of nature, mischief can't hide,
As creatures engage in a game of guess.

The wind tells secrets, a rustle here,
Introducing tickles, a gentle tease.
The trees cheer on with a hearty cheer,
While the critters stumble with ultimate ease.

Through laughter and play, they find their tune,
Under the pines where joy resumes.

Serenity in the Shade

In dappled light, a picnic unfolds,
Sandwiches dance like they are on stage.
Ants join the party, both brave and bold,
Stealing the crumbs, they begin their wage.

A watermelon slice slips from the spread,
Rolling away, it sparks a great chase.
Beneath the shade where mischief is bred,
Laughter erupts at the food's wild race.

The breeze brings whispers of jokes untold,
As tree trunks giggle, their bark worn with age.
Nature's comedy is pure, not controlled,
In the heart of the grove, the stage is the page.

As the sun dips low with a golden blush,
The scene grows merry, a breezy hush.

Solace in the Pine Cone

A pine cone nestled upon a soft bed,
Dreams of being a mighty pine tree.
Instead it rolls underfoot, quite misled,
Only to find itself stuck in a spree.

A playful pup thinks it's a great toy,
Gnawing and tugging, it flings it with grace.
The pine cone bounces, in a whirl of joy,
Landing quite close to a very wet face.

The wet face befriends, with a laugh and a bark,
Together they play, oh what a delight!
In the woods, joy illuminates the dark,
As laughter resounds, and the day turns bright.

All creatures gather, drawn to the fun,
In the laughter of life, there's no need to run.

Conversations with the Canopy

The branches gossip, swaying so free,
While leaves whisper tales into the air.
A woodpecker listens, filled with glee,
He snickers aloud, finding it quite fair.

A chatty bluebird joins with a song,
Singing of adventures in summer's glow.
A squirrel waves like he's part of the throng,
Showing off antics we all ought to know.

"Did you hear of the owl, so wise and bold?"
The trees all nod with a rustling cheer.
"His hoots hold mysteries, ancient and old,
But we'd bet he's lost his glasses, oh dear!"

Under the laughter, the world feels right,
In the chatter of life, from morning to night.

A Stillness of Echoing Pines

Amidst the trees, I stop and stare,
A squirrel darts, my snack laid bare.
I wave goodbye, its cheeky grin,
No chance of sharing this feast within.

The rustling leaves, a giggling sound,
The branches dance, they sway around.
Yet shadows play, they trip my feet,
A comedy act, oh what a feat!

The pine cones drop like heavy stones,
As I dodge them, avoiding groans.
I slip and slide on pine-scented ground,
Nature's slapstick, in laughter, I'm bound.

But don't be fooled by woods so quaint,
There's humor hiding, as sure as paint.
Each twist and turn, a comic show,
In the stillness, the laughter will grow.

Tropical Pine and the Tranquil Light

Under the palms, a tropical tease,
The breeze is light, a gentle breeze.
A picnic spread, all laid with care,
But ants declare war—oh, who'll despair!

The sunlight dances, it flickers and plays,
But I end up sticky in a coconut haze.
I sip my drink, a little too quick,
A splash of humor—it feels like a trick!

The laughter of birds, a surreptitious tune,
As I try to nap under cheerful noon.
But they squawk and dive, it's chaos, I swear,
A party at noon, I'm caught unaware!

Yet friendship blooms in the humid air,
With giggles and grins, I find my share.
In sunlight's glow, the pine trees sway,
And together we laugh, come what may!

Kinship of Fir and Feather

Under the firs, a peculiar pair,
A bird and I, a friendship rare.
He caws and hops, a little too loud,
I try to shush him, but now I'm proud.

Giggles echo through the bending trees,
As we form a band—just him and me.
He sings off-key, oh what a croak,
I join in too, we're both a joke!

With feathers ruffled, he takes a dive,
While I stand still, just trying to jive.
But in this mirth, we share the space,
A joy so silly, a sweet embrace.

When dusk descends on our playful stage,
We laugh out loud, as we turn the page.
A kinship born, through laughter entwined,
Just a bird and a human, whimsically inclined.

The Lantern of the Low-Hanging Boughs

Beneath the boughs, where shadows creep,
I set my lantern, but it starts to leap.
The flame inside, it flickers and spins,
Like a tiny dancer, oh where do I begin?

The branches sway, they beckon me near,
With laughter echoing, it's rather clear.
As I chase my light, it plays hide and seek,
A merry prank, both cheeky and sleek.

But lo! A wiggle, a rustle too,
The lantern dances, away it flew!
I run and trip, oh what a sight,
Under the boughs, it's pure delight!

Yet as I catch it, I burst into glee,
The woods know humor, just like me.
So here I stand, with lantern aglow,
What a fine evening, in laughter we flow!

Secrets Buried in the Pinecone's Hold

A pinecone fell, it made a thud,
Dropped secrets deep within the mud.
Rumor has it, there's treasure found,
But squirrels just laugh, hopping around.

They dig and scratch with all their might,
Finding acorns in their delight.
While searching for gold, they miss the cue,
The truest treasure is a pinecone stew!

With a nutty dance, the critters prance,
Mistaking each twig for a grand romance.
So if you think you've struck it rich,
Just check your pockets—leave that pitch!

For every secret the cone might hide,
There's laughter echoing from inside.
Keep your ears to the ground and listen well,
Nature's spilled jokes, she can't help but tell.

The Gaze Through the Canopy's Veil

Peeking through leaves, the sunbeams wink,
While squirrels and chipmunks silently drink.
A game of hide-and-seek they play,
"Can you find me?" they murmur in a fray.

The branches sway in a silly jig,
Shadows leap like a jolly big pig.
A chipmunk shouts, "Bet you can't see!"
But I've got my binoculars, oh golly gee!

Each gust of wind brings giggles and thrills,
The pine trees whisper all their skills.
True talent shows through a gentle sway,
Nature's humor on full display.

Through the green curtain, we catch a glimpse,
Of nature's jokes and prancing pimps.
So next time you wander where the tall trees sway,
Remember to chuckle along the way.

Whispers Beneath the Needles

Under the needles, secrets unfold,
As the mythical creatures start to mold.
Centuries say the elves play chess,
With pinecone pieces in a fancy dress.

"Checkmate!" calls out the wise old owl,
While the mice all cheer and gently howl.
The trees roll their trunks in a giggly cheer,
As whispers float softly, "What's going on here?"

A shadow darts by with one funny leap,
A raccoon's sneaky visitor, oh so deep!
With a wink and a nod, they plan their heist,
For mushrooms and berries are their main feast.

So next time you wander this green domain,
Listen closely for the laughter it gains.
For beneath the needles, where silence seems nice,
There's humor and chaos—oh, isn't life spice!

Shadows Play in Green

Among the pines, shadows leap and twirl,
In a whimsical dance, they frisky whirl.
A rabbit with rhythm hops left and right,
As if to tell the sun, "I own the night!"

Branches creak and giggle in sly delight,
As fireflies flash, turning dark into light.
A raccoon in shades gives a wink and a grin,
"Care for a dance? Let the fun begin!"

Whispers and chuckles float on the breeze,
As vines stretch and stretch with utmost ease.
The forest is alive with a carnival sound,
A cabaret of life nearby is found.

So come take a stroll, let your worries resound,
Among the tall whispers, pure joy is unbound.
For shadows play tricks in the trees up high,
Just remember to smile and give them a try!

Whispers of the Evergreen

In the woods, a squirrel sneezed,
And startled all the birds that teased.
They laughed and chirped, a feathered choir,
While the breeze played pranks, lifting their attire.

A raccoon donned a hat so tall,
He tripped and tumbled, into a sprawl.
The trees shook with laughter, a rustling cheer,
As critters gathered near, to share the leer.

A frog in rain boots tried to waltz,
But slipped on mud, oh what a false!
The laughter rang through branches high,
While ants in tuxedos queued up nearby.

Beneath bright boughs, the jokes flew wide,
Majestic trees with giggles inside.
In this woodland, oh what a scene,
Where even the pinecones know how to glean.

Beneath the Canopy's Embrace

Under the branches, a party starts,
With acorns bouncing, like playful darts.
A chipmunk juggles with flair and grace,
While clouds of pollen put smiles on every face.

A crow cawed loud, "Who invited the cat?"
The feline laughed, "Just here for a chat!"
But the owl winked with a knowing glance,
And said, "Oh dear, you're taking a chance!"

Dancing pine trees sway right and left,
While the wind plays tunes with cheeky heft.
The bees buzzed jokes, as they gathered their gold,
In a world where laughter is never too old.

Under laughter's shade, all creatures convene,
With stories and giggles, a festive scene.
The nightfall sets in, with a wink and a grin,
As nature's own laughter spreads wide on the skin.

Shadows in the Needlework

Beneath the canopy, shadows waltz,
With giggles echoing, not one thought faults.
The fawn tried to leap, but landed in glee,
Into a patch of dandelion tea.

A wise old owl, with a stern looking stare,
Pretended to snore, while pulling a scare.
A mouse with a violin, played tunes sincere,
And all of the rabbits danced without fear.

The wind whispered secrets to the leaves so green,
As the forest critters formed a lively scene.
With nutty ideas that surely would shine,
The needles of trees shared laughter divine.

Victorious pine cones with crowns made of grass,
Claimed victory for the best comedy class.
Each tree stood proud, their laughter does show,
In shadows and whispers, together they glow.

Songs of the Sylvan Grove

In the grove, a bear held a low-tech phone,
He swiped and giggled, feeling like royalty on a throne.
The trees rolled their eyes, in playful despair,
"Get off the screen, come out for fresh air!"

The woodpecker knocked with a rhythm so bold,
Rounding up critters for stories retold.
With humorous tales and puns to unfurl,
They laughed till the moon gave a twinkling whirl.

A badger in slippers sneaked out for a snack,
But tripped on a twig, went tumbling back.
The laughter erupted, the stars joined in too,
As giggles twinkled in a night sky so blue.

In the sylvan space, friendship ignites,
Where laughter blooms bright, like stars in the nights.
So gather 'round friends, let the fun flow free,
In this great woodland, where joy's the decree.

Twilight Tales in the Woodland Realm

In the dusk, the squirrels chat,
Jokes about a silly cat.
They tease him for his lazy days,
A prince who naps in sunlit rays.

Bunnies hop with giggles near,
While owls hoot, 'What's your fear?'
The raccoons dance on leaves so bright,
With masks they fool the moon at night.

A hedgehog's snore, oh quite a sound,
Making stars spin all around.
The fireflies glow like tiny lamps,
Lighting up the forest camps.

As shadows stretch and whispers creep,
The secrets of the woods, they keep.
In twilight's grip, all jest and fun,
They laugh until the day is done.

Carvings of Time in the Horsehair Whispers

A raccoon with a fancy hat,
Swears he saw a dancing bat.
With horsehair ties, he swings and prances,
Chasing shadows, taking chances.

The pine cones roll, they start to race,
While chipmunks cheer in an acorn space.
The woodpecker drums a silly beat,
As laughter fills the forest street.

A tortoise boasts of winning speed,
But finds himself stuck in a weed.
His friends they chuckle, oh what a sight,
A gentle tease in soft moonlight.

And so they share their silly tales,
In the whispering wind, their joy prevails.
With every laugh, a moment's time,
In horsehair whispers, all feel sublime.

Symphony of the Abiding Pines

When pines hum tunes, it starts to show,
A band of critters in a row.
The chipmunks tap and the badgers sway,
To a melody that leads the way.

A toad croaks out, 'I'm the lead!'
While crickets chirp, 'We're with speed!'
They shake their legs, expect a crowd,
Underneath the pines, so proud.

The foxes play the flutes with flair,
As owls judge with a wise old stare.
Beneath the stars, the symphony grows,
In laughter, the fabled forest glows.

With every note, the night feels young,
As stories mix with songs once sung.
A funny show among the trees,
Creating joy, a gentle breeze.

Wandering Thoughts in the Forest's Fold

As I wander through the foliage wide,
A deer in socks plays hide and slide.
It stumbles, slips, and gives a spin,
'Oh dear,' it sighs, 'let's try again!'

The trees laugh softly, their branches sway,
Offering shade for games they play.
With acorns flying as pearls of zest,
The squirrels launch their little quest.

The bear takes selfies, looking grand,
'This forest life isn't so bland!'
With pixels flashing in the night,
The stars smile down, all looks right.

In this circle of life and cheer,
The forest holds its humor dear.
Wandering thoughts, they twine, entwine,
Creating mischief, oh so fine!

Stillness in the Saplings

The saplings sway with grace and flair,
In breezy gowns, oh, do they dare.
A squirrel snorts, a bird cackles loud,
These tiny trees are quite the crowd.

A twig snaps, a raccoon hops high,
With gangly limbs, they seem to fly.
One pine whispers, 'What's the fuss?'
'Just ground squirrels causing a ruckus!'

When sunlight dances on their heads,
They giggle softly, 'We're not in beds!'
A shadow passes, roots begin to tease,
'Hey, where's the laughter? We need some breeze!'

In their stillness, who could tell,
That each tiny trunk holds a joke to tell?
They plot and chuckle in the shade,
In secret meetings beneath their braid.

The Quiet Retreat

A grove so quiet, folks retreat,
To find a seat, to rest their feet.
Yet up above, the branches swing,
Be careful now, a pinecone's fling!

A passerby, so lost in thought,
Didn't see what the pines had wrought.
With a thud and a comical squeal,
The pinecone drops—a not-so-gentle deal!

The trees snicker, a chorus bright,
'Who knew that pinecones had such might?'
As laughter rustles through the leaves,
The quiet turns into funny reprieves.

So grab a seat and take your time,
Just watch above, avoid the rhyme.
For trees, with wit, hold sly old plays,
In the quiet retreat, where humor stays!

Beneath the Cloak of Green

A blanket green, with humor sewn,
Beneath its cloak, the giggles drone.
A worm tells tales of travels far,
While crooked branches wave like a star!

A deer stumbles, trips on a root,
'That's not my dance!' it claims with hoot.
Meanwhile, the saplings chuckle in glee,
'Oh dear, who taught him that spree?'

With shadows flickering, jokes are spun,
Leaves rustle softly, 'Oh this is fun!'
A pine with sass sports a branchy cap,
'Laughing at life? That's a fine map!'

In these woods where antics reign,
The cloaked greens dance, their joy is plain.
Under the leaves where laughter's free,
Whispers tickle the roots with glee.

A Journey with the Saplings

With sturdy trunks, we take our quest,
A journey led by youthful zest.
The saplings giggle, sprouting high,
'We'll see the world, oh me, oh my!'

Bouncing like bunnies, they chase a breeze,
Pinecones launch with playful ease.
A squirrel flags them for a race,
'Catch me if you can, let's up the pace!'

Roots intertwine as they run the line,
'Watch your step, or you'll hit a vine!'
They frolic on, the laughter grows,
'Is this a forest? Who really knows?'

With leafy crowns, they crown the day,
In a journey paved with fun and play.
Saplings shine with a cheeky twist,
In laughter's grace, none can resist!

An Ode to the Verdant Giants

Oh mighty trees, with limbs so wide,
You hide my socks from the laundry tide.
Your needles drop like confetti rain,
I trip on roots, then laugh through the pain.

Squirrels gossip on branches above,
Claiming the best nuts, oh how they shove!
Your trunk's a stage for birds on high,
They sing so loud, they'd make a cat cry.

In your shade, I rest and dream,
Of ice cream cones and a fishing stream.
Yet here I sit, with ants on my snack,
While you just stand there, not looking back.

So here's to you, you leafy big guys,
With your lofty limbs and curious ties.
If I could dance, I'd twirl around,
But with my two left feet, I'll stay on the ground.

Serenity in the Shade of the Pines

Oh, peaceful pines, how still you stand,
Guardians of secrets in this lush land.
But I must confess, your shade feels nice,
Till sap drips down—now that's not precise!

I try to meditate, but what's that sound?
A woodpecker's ranting, loud and profound.
While I sit cross-legged, oh so zen,
A squirrel's stealing my lunch—again!

In my calm spot, I ponder and muse,
At how you wear a coat of bright hues.
Yet all I want is a quiet retreat,
But you keep giving me pinecone treats.

Oh, nature's charm is quite misconstrued,
When every breeze brings a pine nut feud.
But I shall laugh and take it in stride,
For where else would I find such wild pride?

The Dance of the Forest Spirits

In the pines, I saw spirits whirl,
With wild abandon, they twist and twirl.
But wait, what's this? It's just a bird,
Chasing its tail like I just heard.

Branches sway as if to the beat,
Yet it's just my dog, racing on feet.
He barks at the fairies, or so he thinks,
But all they do is roll their pinks!

With every rustle, I hear a joke,
From shifting shadows, I swear I spoke.
Am I the punchline in their grand play?
Or just uninvited to their ballet?

So here I sit, a bit out of place,
Watching the spirits take flight through space.
In laughter and joy, they twirl and spin,
While I just sip soda and chuckle within.

Tidal Rhythms of the Pine Forest

Waves of green crash, a sight to behold,
With sea breeze whispers, stories retold.
Yet here in the pines, it's more of a giggle,
When I trip on a root—oh, what a wiggle!

The pinecones fall like a clumsy tide,
Bombarding my hat—what a wild ride!
I shake my fist at the skies above,
"Why can't you rain marshmallows I love?"

A picnic spread, I unpack with flair,
But ants have claimed my spot, it's not fair!
With a wave of the hand, I send them away,
Only to find that they've brought friends to play.

So here I feast beneath pine-tree towers,
Watching the antics of nature's powers.
With laughter echoing through branches so vast,
I realize ocean waves can't quite match this blast!

Lullabies of the Pine Fronds

A squirrel danced on my head, oh my,
He chattered jokes and made me cry.
The pine trees swayed with glee, indeed,
As I laughed at my silly, furry friend's speed.

A breeze tickled my nose with flair,
While birds mocked me from the air.
I tried to sing a sweet little tune,
But it sounded more like a cartooned baboon.

Beneath the needles, I stretched out wide,
With a hat full of acorns and a squirrel for a guide.
Oh, what a sight, so funny and rare,
Nature's entertainment, beyond compare.

As the sun set low, the giggles broke loose,
I chuckled at shadows, what a caboose!
Pine fronds whispered, "More fun, my dear!"
And so I stayed, sipping laughter and cheer.

The Tranquil Arms of Nature

In nature's arms, I lay so snug,
But ants decided to give me a shrug.
They marched in straight lines, a tiny parade,
I was the queen, but they wanted my shade.

With each gentle rustle of pine above,
Came whispers of secrets and also a shove.
A creature peeked out, it gave me a wink,
I laughed so hard, fell face-first in the drink.

The ground was soft with a spongy layer,
Where my laughs bounced back like a wise old player.
I tossed up a wish, now wouldn't it be fine,
To giggle like this for the rest of the time?

Oh, the charms of green, how they do twirl,
With squirrels prancing in a raucous whirl.
I found my peace in this uproarious scene,
Nature's humor is the best ever seen.

Light Filtering Through the Firs

Under the furs, where shadows play,
The light dances on like a silly ballet.
I tripped on a root, oh what a sight,
Like nature's grand jester, oh what a fright!

The sunbeam tickled my nose, how it gleamed,
I lost my cool and loudly screamed.
The birds cawed back like they were in on it,
Challenging me to a sky-high skit.

A rabbit hopped by with a wiggle and grin,
Wearing a bow tie, rather dapper within.
It winked and said, "You're a riot, my friend!"
Together we giggled, no need to pretend.

With each golden ray, and chirps in the air,
I felt like a fool, light as a feather.
Oh, what joy found in nature's embrace,
A weird little rendezvous in this happy place.

Murs and Murmurs of Woodland

In the woods, where whispers collide,
The trees hold secrets, giggles inside.
A brush of fur, a flash, and a dart,
Nature's own jesters, they play their part.

Murmurs of laughter weave in the trees,
While chipmunks prance with the greatest of ease.
They tell tales of mischief and bits of fun,
Chasing their shadows till the day is done.

With each rustle, my heart skips a beat,
What antics await, oh what a treat!
From the canopy down to the roots,
Laughter lives on, in all of nature's suits.

So here I am, enchanted and free,
Surrounded by giggles, just nature and me.
In the murmur of branches and soft pecan,
I'm wrapped in the warmth of woodland charm.